...IF YOU LIVED WITH
•THE SIOUX INDIANS•

by Ann McGovern
illustrated by Beatrice Darwin

SCHOLASTIC INC.
New York Toronto London Auckland Sydney

The author acknowledges with thanks
the invaluable assistance given by
Frederick J. Dockstader, Director,
The Museum of the American Indian
Heye Foundation

ISBN 0-590-40533-0

Reading level is determined by using the Spache Readability Formula. 3.2 signifies high 3rd grade level.

12 11 10 9 8 7 6 5 4 3 2 1   6 7 8 9/8

for Peter, Charles, Annie, and Jim

CONTENTS

Introduction

Indians were the first people to live in what is now the United States.

By 1776, when the United States became a nation, there were about 250 different tribes living in different parts of the country.

There was no such thing as *one* Indian way of life. Each tribe lived in its own way. Different tribes lived in different kinds of houses, wore different clothes, ate different food, and played different games.

Most of this book tells about the way the Sioux tribe lived for fifty years — from

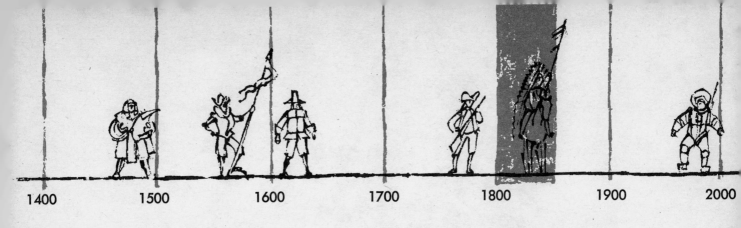

1400   1500   1600   1700   1800   1900   2000

1800 (twenty-four years after the United States became a nation) until 1850 (when the white settlers came West by the thousands). Those fifty years were exciting times — when the Sioux rode horses to hunt the buffalo that roamed the western plains. The end of the book tells about the way the Sioux Indians live today.

Look at the time line on this page. The part that is in color shows the years this book is mostly about.

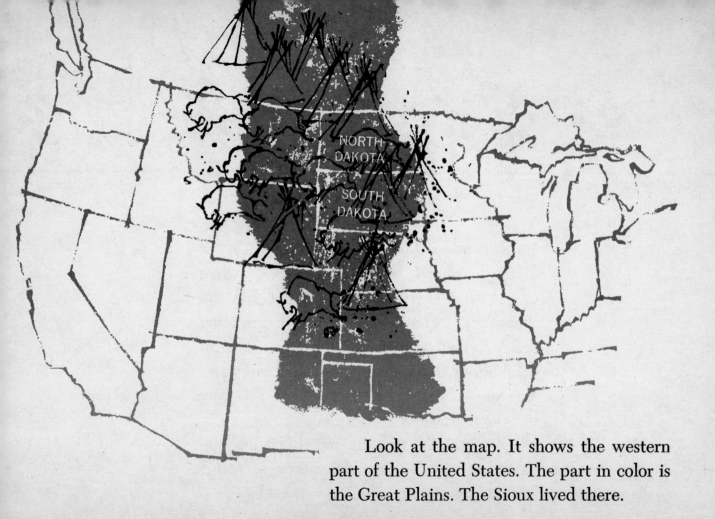

NORTH DAKOTA

SOUTH DAKOTA

Look at the map. It shows the western part of the United States. The part in color is the Great Plains. The Sioux lived there.

They lived in what is now North Dakota and South Dakota. Dakota was another name for the Sioux tribe.

At that time, there were thirty-one tribes on the Great Plains alone. All these Indians are Plains Indians. The Sioux tribe was the most famous of all the Plains Indians.

The Sioux Indians still live in the West today. About 40,000 Sioux Indians are living today in North Dakota and South Dakota.

The way they live today is very different from the way their great-great-great-grandparents used to live.

What was it like to be a Sioux Indian long ago? What was it like living in a tipi? Did boys and girls have time to play? What clothes did they wear? This book tells you.

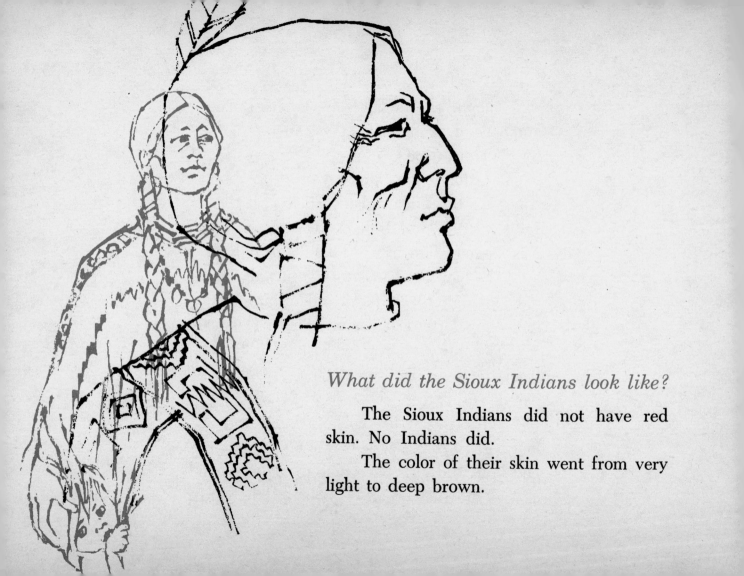

What did the Sioux Indians look like?

The Sioux Indians did not have red skin. No Indians did.

The color of their skin went from very light to deep brown.

The name redskin came from the red paint the Indians used on their faces when they went to war.

Most Sioux Indians were tall and thin. Boys and girls, men and women wore their hair long. Their thick, dark hair came down to their shoulders. Sometimes they wore their hair loose and sometimes they wore it in braids.

They parted their hair down the middle and sometimes they painted the part line red.

To keep their hair neat, they rubbed buffalo fat or bear fat into it.

If you lived with the Sioux, what kind of house would you live in?

You would live in a tent, called a *tipi*. (Say: TEE-pee.) Your tipi would be made of tall wooden poles covered with buffalo hides. The buffalo hides were so tough they lasted 25 years — through winter storms and summer heat.

The tipi had only one room. If you had many brothers and sisters, your mother would make a bigger tipi.

Bare earth would be your floor. At night you could look up and see the stars through the two flaps at the top of the tipi. When it rained or snowed, the flaps were closed. In a Sioux tipi, you would be warm in the winter and cool in the summer.

When the Sioux moved from place to place, they took their tipis along. A tipi could be taken apart in minutes and quickly set up again.

Women were in charge of the tipis. When it was time to move, women took their tipis apart. And when the tribe set up camp again, women put the tipis up. Three or four women working together could put up a tipi in a few minutes.

Would you live in the same place all the time?

No. You would live in different places. The Sioux Indians had to keep on the move to hunt the buffalo that roamed the plains. When the Sioux Indians traveled, they took everything they had with them.

You wouldn't travel much in winter months. It was freezing cold. And besides, when the buffalo were covered with snow, it was hard to find them. It was hard to see a snow-covered buffalo against the snow-covered plains.

How would you travel?

The entire village traveled together. First the women took down all the tipis. Then everything was piled together — tipi poles, tipi covers, robes, clothing, tools, and dried food.

Everything was put onto a *travois* (TRAV-WAH) — two long poles, with short poles across it to hold the loads. Dogs dragged the travois. Later horses were used too.

The chiefs rode in front, with the hunters. The women and the girls walked behind, carrying the household goods. Babies rode in cradles, tied to their mothers' backs.

One-year-old boys would be held on the horses, in front of their fathers, so they would get used to the feel of riding.

Boys had the most fun. They raced their horses, shouting and showing off. If the boys got too noisy, a member of the *tokala* would ask them to stop. The tokala was a group of Indian men chosen to keep order on the trip.

Would you stay close to your tipi?

You wouldn't have to. You would be free to wander anywhere in the village.

You might visit the tipi of your second mother and father. When a Sioux baby was born, his parents chose another set of parents to help care for him. The second mother and father might be the baby's grandparents. Or they might be friends of the family.

The second father would be chosen because he had some special skill to teach the boy. He might be an excellent hunter or a warrior or a medicine man.

The second mother was expected to be gentle and loving and to help teach the girl.

You would spend as much time with your second parents as you would with your own mother and father.

The Sioux Indians believed in sharing everything they had. So if you were wandering about and you got tired, someone would give you a place to sleep. If you were hungry, someone would feed you. And if you were sad, someone would listen to you and comfort you.

In your tipi, too, there would always be extra food in the cooking pot. There would be an extra soft buffalo robe for a sleepy head. And there would be a kind word for anyone passing by.

Where would you sleep?

Your bed would be a buffalo robe. It would be so soft and so thick you would not feel the hard ground beneath you. In winter, the thick robe would keep you warm.

A buffalo robe was too heavy for the summer. Your summer bed would be a soft deerskin.

Everyone in the family slept on the left side of the door. The space to the right of the door was kept for company.

Babies slept in their cradles hung from poles, high above the floor. During the day, the cradles were hung on tree branches. Babies were rocked to sleep by the gentle breezes.

What would you eat?

Buffalo, buffalo, buffalo, and more buffalo. Buffalo boiled, buffalo broiled, dried buffalo, and sometimes raw buffalo. You would even drink the blood of buffalo!

To boil buffalo blood, the women threw hot stones into the stomach of a freshly killed buffalo!

After a buffalo hunt, everyone had plenty of fresh buffalo meat to eat. In the winter when it was hard to hunt, they ate dried buffalo meat called *pemmican*.

After each big hunt, the women would take some of the buffalo meat. They cut the meat into thin strips and hung the strips on racks to dry in the sun. Then they pounded the dry meat until it was like

powder. They added wild cherries — pits, too — and mixed it with melted buffalo fat. The pemmican was stuffed into flat rawhide bags and stored for winter.

You would eat other meat besides buffalo. You would eat bear, deer, antelope, and sometimes wild turkeys and hens. Sioux Indians didn't like to eat rabbit or squirrel very often, and they hardly ever ate fish.

Sometimes you would eat fruits and vegetables. The Sioux did not plant gardens because they were always on the move and could not take care of them. They picked wild fruits — cherries, berries, and plums. And they dug up wild vegetables — potatoes, spinach, and prairie turnips.

If someone in the Sioux tribe had enough food, no one in the Sioux tribe went hungry — for food was shared by all.

What kind of clothes would you wear?

Do you think men always wore tall feather headdresses? Do you think women always wore beaded dresses? Well, they didn't.

Only a few men owned the tall feather headdress. And they wore it only at special times. Most of the time, a Sioux wore nothing on his head except a strip of leather to keep his hair back.

Sioux Indians did not have glass beads at all until the white men brought them to use in trading. Before that they decorated their clothing with leather fringes, quills from porcupines, or paint.

Clothes were made from animal skins — deerskins, mostly. For every day, women and girls wore long dresses and leggings. They saved their decorated dresses for special times. Their special clothes might be decorated with elk teeth, bear claws, feathers, and fur.

Sioux men wore loose deerskin shirts and tight leggings. In warm weather and when they were hunting or fighting, they wore only a strip of leather, called a breech-cloth, and a pair of moccasins. Boys did not wear any clothing in warm weather until they were eight years old.

In the winter, a buffalo robe would keep you warm. Boys and girls wore robes made from young buffalo calves. You wore the robe with the fur side inside. Your winter moccasins would be lined with fur too. You never wore socks or underwear. In the winter, men and boys wore two or three shirts — one on top of the other. And women and girls wore two or three dresses at one time.

Women made all the clothing for their families. They made clothing from the softened skins of elk, deer, or antelope.

Did Sioux children go to school?

There were no special schools for children. Learning time was all the time. You learned as you played. You learned as you helped your parents with all the work.

The best hunters and warriors were chosen to teach the boys. Boys learned how to make arrows and how to shoot them. They learned how to hunt, how to ride their horses without a saddle, and how to steal horses from enemies.

By the time a boy was five, he was a good rider. And at seven, he could take care of the family horses.

Contests were held to see how much the boys had learned. The boys who did the best were picked to ride out with the scouts or to run errands for the warriors in a battle.

Before a Sioux girl could marry, she had to know how to make leather from animal skins, how to make and repair clothing and tipis, how to cook, and how to care for a baby.

She learned to paint beautiful designs and to decorate with porcupine quills. She practiced her quill work by decorating moccasins for her brothers.

Did boys and girls learn the same things?

Both boys and girls learned to swim before they learned to walk. And they both learned to ride a horse at an early age too. Before they were five, girls and boys could hunt small animals with a bow and arrow.

But after the age of five, girls began to learn the work of their mothers and boys started to do the things the men did.

What would your very first lesson be?

You would learn your very first lesson in the very first hour of your life. Newborn babies learned how not to cry out loud.

As soon as you made a crying sound, your mother would gently pinch your nose and put her hand over your mouth. Every time you began to cry, she did this. Soon you would learn not to cry out loud.

Why was this lesson so important? Suppose you hurt yourself when you were out on a buffalo hunt. If you cried out loud, the buffalo would run away, the hunt would be spoiled, and the tribe would have no meat.

Suppose you cried out loud when your tribe was hiding from the enemy. Your loud cry would give away the tribe's hiding place.

Were grownups strict?

Indians did not spank their children or yell at them. They did not tell them over and over again what to do.

If a child went too close to the fire, no one would cry out to stop him. A child would find out for himself that fire burns.

Of course, if he were about to fall into the fire, you can be sure that a grownup would pull him back.

Sioux children learned many things by finding out for themselves what was dangerous and what was not.

How did the Sioux hunt the buffalo?

Each hunt was carefully planned at a council meeting. The chiefs chose the leaders of the hunt. They chose men who would keep order. They chose scouts to ride out and find the huge herd of buffalo. Some men were chosen to do the hunting for other members of the tribe — for those who were too old or too sick to hunt for themselves.

It might take the scouts weeks before they found buffalo. Meanwhile, everyone in camp was busy. It was a time for playing games, dancing, and singing. It was a time for worshipping. It was a time for visiting friendly tribes nearby and trading with them.

When the scouts returned with the news that a buffalo herd was found, the camp moved. They wanted to be as close to the buffalo herd as possible.

On the day of the hunt, every hunter mounted his horse.

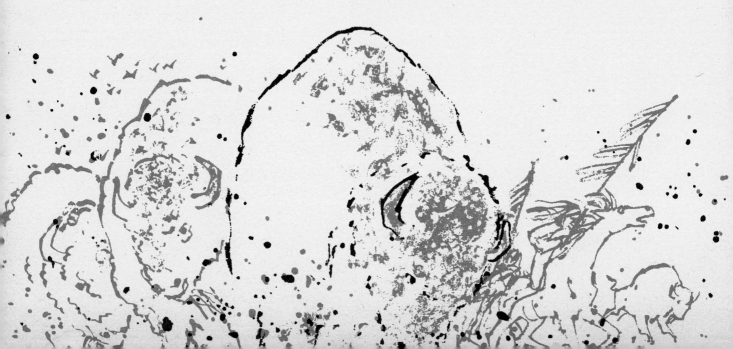

At a signal from the chief, the men charged. The buffalo began to run, making clouds of dust. The hunters aimed their arrows at the buffalo's heart. The buffalo ran so fast the hunters had time to shoot only three arrows before the stop-shooting signal was given. A buffalo hunt took about ten minutes.

No one was allowed to kill more buffalo than the tribe could use.

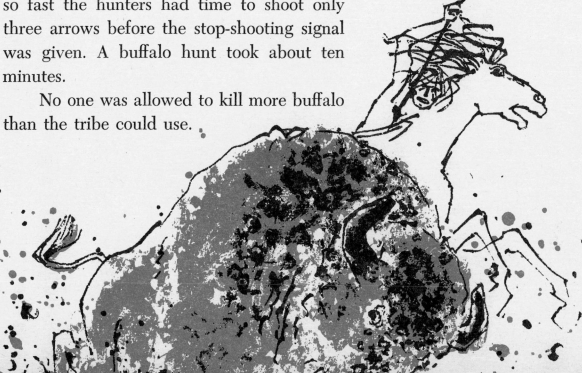
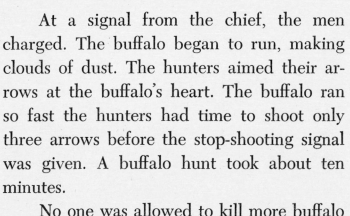

There was more than one way to hunt buffalo.
Here the Sioux are driving buffalo
over a steep cliff.

Did boys take part in the hunt?

Hunting buffalo was dangerous. A boy might get knocked over by a charging buffalo. A horse might fall and throw a boy right into the middle of the stampeding buffalo.

It was too dangerous for boys to ride with the hunters. But they were allowed to tag along far behind the hunters. The boys rode their own colts. With their bows and arrows, they shot the young buffalo calves that followed the herd.

Boys were expected to hunt their first buffalo calf before they were ten years old.

What happened after the hunt?

The women followed the hunters with their pack horses. The men helped the women skin the buffalo, cut up the meat, and load it on the horses.

They all rode back to the camp and the fun and feasting began.

If a boy had hunted his first buffalo, his family might give him a feast — but he would not be allowed to eat any of the buffalo meat himself! That was to teach him it was wrong to want things for himself alone.

Songs were made up and sung in his honor. And his family might hold a *give-away*. A give-away was like a birthday party — but the gifts were given to the guests!

After the give-away, the boy's family wouldn't have much left. They knew that sooner or later the guests would bring gifts back to them. But what about the things they needed right away? The family had to get busy and make them.

What could you make out of a buffalo?

You could make many meals out of buffalo meat.

And most every part of the buffalo was used for something.

Shields were made from the hump of the buffalo.

Toys and tools were made from the bones of the buffalo. A special kind of needle, called an awl, was sometimes made from buffalo bones too. Some bones made good painting sticks.

The muscles along the buffalo's backbone, called sinew, were used as thread in sewing. Twisted sinew made strong bows.

Spoons and cups were made from the horns of the buffalo.

The stomach of the buffalo was cleaned out and made a fine pot. It was also used for carrying food and water.

The tongue of the buffalo was special. It was saved for important ceremonies — special religious celebrations.

Dried buffalo droppings were used for fuel for camp fires.

Buffalo hair was used for making ropes, fancy belts, and decorations.

Buffalo ribs made sleds for winter fun.

A very important part of the buffalo was its hide. There were two ways of preparing buffalo hides. One way made hard leather, called rawhide. Rawhide was nearly as tough as wood. The other way — tanning the hides — made leather nearly as soft as cloth. Soft hides were used to make moccasins, clothing, pipe holders, and tipis.

Rawhide had a hundred uses. It was used to make drums, rattles, and bags to hold dried meat and clothing. Glue was made by boiling rawhide. Rawhide was even used for making splints for broken bones!

Did the Sioux Indians work hard?

Everyone had to work hard. Everything the Sioux had or used they had to make themselves.

The women did all the cooking and made all the clothing from animal skins. Women used porcupine quills to decorate clothing and bags.

The men did all the hunting. But first they had to make bows and arrows, spears and shields.

Men and women decorated tipis, shields, and all kinds of cases that held all kinds of things.

Women painted designs on them. But they never painted pictures of people or of animals. Only men did that kind of artwork.

Was there time for fun?

Everyone played games. Games for boys trained them to be good hunters and warriors.

There were races on foot and races on horseback. There were contests in running and jumping and in shooting arrows.

Everyone played ball — girls, too. But boys played rougher. They played hitting, running, and throwing games.

In the winter, boys and girls would spin homemade tops on the ice and go sliding in sleds made of buffalo ribs.

Winter nights were good for storytelling. It was hard to choose a favorite story. Would you want to hear a real adventure tale or a spooky folk tale?

There were games for indoors too. Everyone in the family played guessing games indoors. A favorite was *moccasin*. Three moccasins were set out. A small pebble was put into one of the three. Someone had to guess which moccasin held the pebble.

When Indians played games, they made bets on who would win. Sometimes they bet everything they had. If they lost, they lost their shirt, their horses — even their tipi!

What was the Sioux religion?

The Sioux believed that everything had a life of its own. They believed that there were rock spirits, tree spirits, and cloud spirits. They believed that the spirits could change their shapes to become animals or people — or that they had the power to be invisible.

They believed that the earth was the mother of all the spirits. They believed that the sun had great power, for it gave light and warmth. There were also spirits for the four directions — east, west, north, and south. And there were spirits for the earth and the sky.

The greatest power, they thought, was *Wakan Tanka,* or the Great Spirit. *Wakan Tanka* sent them buffalo.

The Sioux believed that dreams and signs came to them from the spirits — dreams and signs that would bring them good luck and keep away sickness.

The Sioux believed that after a man died, he would live with the spirits forever. He would go on doing the same things that he had done on earth.

How did the Sioux worship?

Every day the Sioux worshipped the spirits they believed in.

They prayed and they sang to the spirits. They danced and gave gifts to the spirits. Sometimes they did these things alone. And sometimes the whole tribe worshipped together and held a ceremony.

The most famous ceremony was the Sun Dance. It took place every year, before the big buffalo hunt. It lasted many days. Everybody took part to ask the spirits to bring them plenty of buffalo.

As part of the ceremony, a few of the men tortured themselves. They believed that would please the spirits. Then they asked the spirits to take pity on them.

Everything the Sioux did, they did to please the spirits. The way they ate, smoked their pipes, painted their faces, even the way they placed their tipis was to please the spirits. They set their tipis around in a circle, because they believed that all round things had special powers.

What was the most important time in a boy's life?

When a Sioux boy was about twelve years old, it was time for him to seek the spirit that would protect him for the rest of his life.

He would see the spirit in a dream. The Sioux called this kind of dream a vision.

First, a little house, called a sweat lodge, was built. Stones were heated over fires. Then water was poured over the hot stones. Soon the little house was filled with steam. The boy stayed in the hot sweat lodge and prayed. Then he went to a brook and jumped into the cold water.

Next, the boy was taken to a place far from his village and left there alone. For four days and four nights, he did not eat or drink anything. For four days and nights he prayed to the spirits. He prayed for the spirits to send him special signs.

He had to remember what he saw in his dreams.

After four days, the boy was very hungry, very thirsty, and very weak. He could hardly stand up. Some men from his tribe brought him back to the village. He was taken to a holy man — a medicine man.

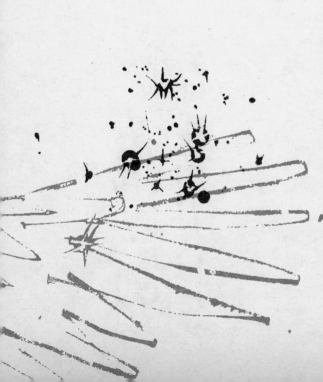

He told the medicine man everything he had heard, seen, and felt. He told the medicine man everything he had seen in his dreams.

The medicine man could tell from the signs and from the boy's dreams what his special spirit was. It might be a bear or a fox or an eagle. The boy's spirit would protect him always and keep him from harm.

If a boy had seen an eagle in his dreams, that meant he would have the fine eyesight of an eagle. He would be able to attack his enemies as swiftly as an eagle too.

The boy would paint special signs of the eagle on his tipi and on his shield. He would make up songs and dances to his spirit.

Then there would be a feast — a feast to celebrate a boy who was ready to take his place among the men.

Did girls have a special ceremony too?

Before a girl was old enough to get married, she, too, had to know what her special spirit was. She would see her spirit in a vision — just the way the boy saw his spirit.

But a girl would not have to spend four days and nights alone. An old woman of the tribe would stay with her.

The girl did not go hungry or thirsty. She could eat and drink a little. During the four days she had to pray and she had to work. She had to make leather from skins, sew, cook, and chop wood.

After four days, the women of the tribe came and took her to the medicine man. He told her the meaning of her dreams and what her spirit was.

That night, the women bathed her and dressed her in fine new clothes.

A feast followed. People gave the girl many presents. They danced and sang to celebrate a girl who was ready to take her place among the women.

What is a medicine bundle?

A Sioux believed that many things kept danger away — his prayers, dances, and songs to his spirit. His *medicine bundle* was most important: A Sioux made his own medicine bundle and the only other person who knew what was in it was the medicine man.

The medicine man told him what to put into the leather bag — things that would please the spirit. It might be an eagle feather or a tooth of an animal or a special pipe.

If a man was having bad luck, he might look for another medicine bundle. He might go to a man who was having good luck and ask to borrow the lucky man's medicine bundle. He would have to pay a lot for it — maybe as much as two horses.

Every Sioux believed his war shield had special powers, too. No one was allowed to use another man's shield without permission.

In good weather the shield hung outside the tipi. The women of the tipi were very careful not to let it touch the ground.

How did a Sioux get a wife?

Before a man could get married, he had to have many horses. And he had to win honors by being brave in war and in the hunt. It took a long time to get many honors and horses. Often a man was not ready to marry until he was twenty-five.

It was no secret which girl a Sioux wanted to marry. Whenever the girl was picking berries or carrying water home, there he would be!

At night the young man stood outside the girl's tipi for hours. He might not be the only man who wanted to marry her. There might be six others standing outside her tipi too!

Later, if one of the young men thought he had a chance, he would come to her tipi and play songs to her on his wooden flute.

If the young man was sure the girl liked him, he would bring a horse to her family. If the family accepted the horse, it meant the girl wanted to marry him too.

Then could the young man ask the girl to marry him? No, he could not do the asking himself. An old lady of the tribe had to ask for him. Then he had to give the family many more horses.

Where did the bride and bridegroom live after they were married?

They lived near the wife's parents. Sometimes they moved into her parents' tipi. And sometimes the wife's mother moved in with them!

Always, some older person would come to live with them. In this way, the young couple had the help and advice of an older person, and no old person ever went without a home in the Sioux tribe.

Sioux men sometimes had more than one wife — if they were rich enough to take care of more than one woman. Often the new wife would be the first wife's cousin or sister.

Then the first wife would have another woman in the tipi to help with the work.

What were good manners?

If a stranger came to your tipi, you would greet him with a word or two. Then the two of you would sit quietly and not say another word for a long time. It was good manners to be quiet.

You would never, never show how you felt in front of a stranger. Even if you were angry or sad, your face would not show it.

If someone in your tribe died, people did show sorrow. They cut their own skin until it bled. They cried and sobbed in public. But it was bad manners to ever again say the name of the dead person.

It was bad manners for a boy to laugh and joke with his sisters or his mother. But there were other people in your family you were *supposed* to laugh and joke with. It would be bad manners if you didn't.

It was good manners for a Sioux to share everything he had with everyone. Any stranger was invited to share the family's pipe and food. He could even share their clothing if he needed it.

What happened if someone got sick?

The Indians were good doctors. They knew how to make medicines, how to heal cuts and wounds, and how to fix broken bones.

If you broke a bone, you would need a splint made of rawhide. First your mother would soak a piece of rawhide in water. Then she would wrap it around your broken bone. Soon the rawhide would shrink and harden into a fine splint.

The Indians used plants called herbs to make medicines. Doctors today use many of the same herbs.

Sometimes the herbs did not make a sick person better. Then the medicine man, known as a *shaman,* was called in.

The Indians believed the shaman had special powers to cure the sick. He showed his power by singing songs and dancing to the spirits.

Often a shaman could cure only one type of sickness. There were shamans to cure arrow wounds and shamans to cure snake bites.

Hops   Mint   Sage   Lambs-quarters

If a child was very sick, the shaman might change the child's name. That was said to be a good cure.

If a sick person did not get better, the Indians would not blame the shaman. Perhaps the sick person had not followed instructions, they thought.

But Sioux Indians hardly ever got sick. They were very healthy until the white man came. Then the Indians caught diseases from the white man that they had never known before — sicknesses like scarlet fever, measles, smallpox, tuberculosis, and sore throats. The Indians became very sick. More Indians died from the white man's diseases than from his bullets.

How did the Sioux talk to other Indians?

Many different tribes of Indians lived on the Great Plains. Each tribe had its own language. So how did they understand each other?

They used sign language. They moved their hands and fingers in certain ways to make signs — signs that everyone understood.

If you met an Indian from another tribe, you would be able to tell him about the last buffalo hunt — even though both of you spoke different languages. You would tell him by signs and he would understand.

The Sioux Indians did not make smoke signals.

Did the Sioux like war?

From the time they were little, Sioux men were taught that war was like a wonderful game. It was a time for every man to win honors.

Most of their wars were not dangerous. For the Sioux did not go to war to kill or to capture prisoners or to take land away from other tribes.

Most of the time they went to war to get horses. If the Sioux lost a fight, they might go to war again, just to try and get even.

But the most important reason for a man to fight was to win honors for himself.

Before they went to war they prayed to the spirits for victory. They painted their faces and bodies, and sometimes their horses. They used red paint, for strength and courage.

When the white men came, the Sioux way of fighting changed. The white men fought to take over Indian land. The white men were ready to kill.

For the Sioux Indians, war could no longer be a wonderful game. Now the Sioux had to fight for their very lives.

*What was the bravest thing
a Sioux could do?*

The bravest thing a Sioux could do was to touch an enemy during a battle and not hurt him.

That took more courage than shooting the enemy with a bow and arrow. With a

bow and arrow, you did not have to come close to your enemy at all!

Another brave act was to creep into an enemy camp and cut loose a horse that was tied up.

Every man kept count of the brave things he did and how many times he did them. This came to be called *counting coup*. (Say: coo.) Coup is a French word meaning hit or strike.

During a battle, every Sioux carried a special stick with him — a *coup stick*. The first man to touch a living enemy with his coup stick could count a *first coup*. A first coup was the highest honor a man could win.

Three other men could touch the same man and earn the right to count coup too. But second, third, or fourth coups did not count as much as the first coup.

Did the Sioux Indians scalp their enemies?

At one time or another, all Plains Indians took scalps. But a Sioux would scalp only an enemy who was already dead.

The Sioux felt that there was special meaning in an enemy's scalp. It was round like the sun, so for the Sioux it had power, like the sun. When a Sioux took a scalp, it was as if he were taking on extra power.

A Sioux kept a scalp all his life, the way a soldier of today might keep his medals.

What weapons did the Sioux use?

Every Sioux had a good spear, a war club, and a strong bow with many arrows.

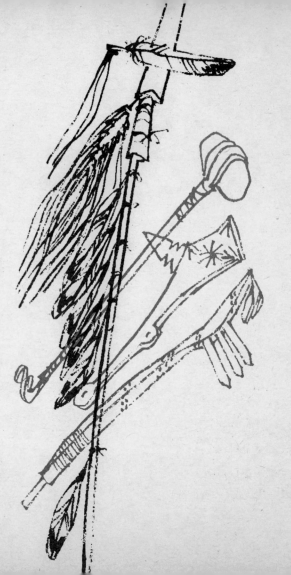

Every man's arrows were marked or painted in a different way. Then every man could keep track of his own arrows and what he shot.

But the most important weapon to the Sioux was his shield. It was round, and so for the Sioux it had special powers. And it was painted with designs the spirits sent to each man through his dreams.

If a Sioux should lose his shield, he felt he could no longer fight. He felt that his powers were taken away from him.

What happened after a battle?

The Sioux showed off. They loved to brag about their brave deeds. And everyone loved to listen.

After a victory, there was a celebration. Everyone put on his best clothes. The men painted their faces and bodies black.

A pole was set up. Each man got up and called out the brave deeds he had done that day. For each brave deed, he struck the pole with his coup stick.

He could wear a feather for each brave deed too. If a man had many feathers, he could put them on a war bonnet. Only a few men ever got to wear a big war bonnet.

Old men loved to tell about their brave deeds of long ago. It didn't matter how many times their stories had been told. The people shouted their applause as loudly as if they were hearing the stories for the first time.

Could anyone become an Indian chief?

No girl ever grew up to become an Indian chief.

But any boy could hope to. A tribe had many chiefs — all leaders.

A chief was not a king. A boy did not become a chief just because his father was a chief.

A boy would have to grow up to be a brave man. He would have to lead many battles and steal many horses.

Most chiefs gave away everything they had. Chiefs gave many feasts and at the feasts, they gave away their horses and their buffalo robes. You could not become a chief unless you were known to be generous.

Could a chief make a rule by himself?

No. The chiefs met together, in a meeting called a council. Together, they made the rules for the tribe.

There were rules for times of peace and other rules for times of war.

In time of war, the chiefs chose a brave young man to be war chief. The war chief would be the leader of one battle only. When the battle was over, his job as war chief was over too.

What happened to a Sioux who broke the rules of the tribe?

A Sioux who broke the rules was punished. The chiefs of the tribe decided what the punishment should be.

A man who broke the rules might have his tipi burned. Or he might be whipped in front of the whole tribe.

Another punishment was to make a man leave the tribe for a year or so. The man could take his tipi, some clothes, and an old horse.

This was cruel punishment. Sioux Indians were used to sharing the things they had and the work they did. So it was very hard for a man to have to live alone.

Being laughed at was the punishment for lying! Girls and women would laugh at a man who did not tell the truth. They would make him feel ashamed in front of the tribe.

Who were the other important men in the tribe?

The medicine man, or shaman, was an important man. His main job was to cure the sick. His special powers made him important in ceremonies.

The crier was another important man. He rode through the tribe, calling out news of war, of the hunt, of feasts, weddings, and ceremonies.

A *heyoka* made people laugh. A *heyoka* was a clown and everything he did was backward. He said yes when he meant no. He acted cold on a hot day. He rode his horse backward and he walked on his hands.

If you wanted to be a *heyoka*, you would have to become part of a *heyoka* society. You would have to follow certain rules the society made.

Who owned Sioux land?

The Sioux believed that no one owned the land. How could land be owned? Land came from *Wakan Tanka*—the Great Spirit. The sky and the waters came from the Great Spirit, too. Could the sky be owned? Could the great sea be owned?

You could own your horse, your clothes, your tipi and everything in it. You could sell your things if you wanted to. You could give them away.

But not land. And since no one owned the land, no one could sell the land.

But then the white men came and wanted the land. They gave the Indians some money and said the land was now theirs.

But the Indians thought they were renting land to the white men, for just a little while.

Land was for the tribe to use forever, the way it had always been used, they thought.

What happened to the Sioux when the white men came?

The white men came with promises. They said that the Sioux could live in the beautiful Black Hills of South Dakota forever. But the promises were broken. The Indians were tricked. They lost their homes.

The white men came with guns to shoot the buffalo and soon the buffalo were gone. Thousands of Sioux went hungry.

The white men came with strange, new germs, and soon thousands of Indians took sick and died.

The white men came with whiskey. The Indians never had whiskey before. It made them sick. It made them act crazy. It turned friends into enemies and made brothers fight each other.

The white men came with their ideas about how the Sioux should live. They wanted the Sioux to farm land, but the Sioux did not know how to be farmers. The white men wanted the Sioux to worship the way they did. The government said the Sioux could no longer have their most important ceremony — the Sun Dance.

By 1860, just before Abraham Lincoln became President, 150,000 settlers had taken over the land where the Sioux had lived — the land the Sioux believed could never be owned.

**A note from the author
about the Sioux Indians today**

The Sioux had a great and glorious past. When the settlers took over Indian land, the Sioux were forced to move to reservations — land set aside for Indians to live on.

Little by little, every bit of good land was taken away from the Sioux.

Today, many Sioux Indians live in cities. But most Sioux Indians still live on reservations in North Dakota and South Dakota — reservations managed by the government.

The land on the reservations is poor. It is only good for grazing cattle. But not many Indians have money for cows and horses.

Today, more and more Sioux leaders are speaking out.

The Indians were here, they say — and happy here — long before the settlers came. Now the Indians have only the poorest land to live on. And they have not been given a fair chance.

They are saying that they don't want the government to manage things for them. They want to decide for themselves how they will live.

They must have better houses for their people. They must have better schools for their children. There must be more doctors and nurses and hospitals.

Today, more and more young people are going away to college so they can return to the reservations as doctors and lawyers and teachers, to help their tribe.

The Sioux Indians of today are still doing some of the things their great-grand-parents did.

Once again the Sun Dance is given every summer. Thousands of Indians come hundreds of miles to take part in a *powwow*. There are parades, dances, and contests to judge the best dancing and costumes. The next day, the families of the winners hold a give-away as in the old days.

There are still a few families who dry meat and make clothing from animal skins, as in the old days.

The Sioux Indians have never lost their wonderful ways of sharing. No matter how poor a family may be, they still would not let a stranger leave their tribe hungry.

The Sioux are proud of their wonderful past. They want their children to know about it and they want them to be able to speak the Sioux language. The Sioux Indians want their children to learn everything other American children learn. And they want everyone to know the true story of their glorious past.